ABOVE: *Lancashire loom weaving inside a Rochdale mill, about 1900.*

COVER: *The Lady of Shalott weaves tapestry pictures on her loom.*

> *But in her web she still delights*
> *To weave the mirror's magic sights,*
> *For often thro' the silent nights*
> *A funeral, with plumes and lights*
> *And music, went to Camelot:*
> *Or when the moon was overhead,*
> *Came two lovers lately wed;*
> *'I am half sick of shadows', said*
> *The Lady of Shalott.*

*Verse by Alfred, Lord Tennyson, 1842. Painting, 'The Lady of Shalott' (part 2), 1915, by John William Waterhouse. (Art Gallery of Ontario, Toronto. Gift of Mrs Phillip B. Jackson, 1917.)*

# LOOMS AND WEAVING

## Anna Benson and Neil Warburton

A Shire book

# CONTENTS

Published in 2002 by Shire Publications Ltd, Cromwell House, Church Street, Princes Risborough, Buckinghamshire HP27 9AA, UK. Copyright © 1986 by Anna Benson and Neil Warburton. First published 1986; reprinted 1990, 1995 and 2002. Shire Album 154. ISBN 0 85263 753 5. All rights reserved.

Printed in Great Britain by CIT Printing Services Ltd, Press Buildings, Merlins Bridge, Haverfordwest, Pembrokeshire SA61 1XF.

British Library Cataloguing in Publication Data: Benson, Anna P. Looms and weaving.—(Shire album; 154). 1. Weaving — History. I. Title. II. Warburton, Neil. 677'.028242. TS1490-1500. ISBN 0-85263-753-5.

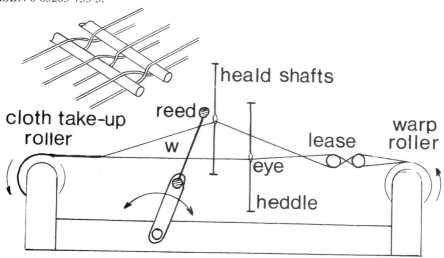

ABOVE: *Weaving on a table loom. All the warp threads are wound on the back roller and each thread is taken around the lease-rods (shown in the inset, top left), through the eye in the heald, through the comb-like reed and fixed to the cloth take-up roller at the front of the loom. Weaving takes place by passing weft threads (W) through the space or shed created by lifting chosen heald shafts. After each pick of weft the reed beats the yarn up to the edge, or fell, of the cloth. Crossing alternate warp threads into a figure-of-eight creates a 'lease' which helps to keep the threads parallel, enables the weaver to locate broken warp ends and acts as a guide when passing successive threads in regular order through the heddle eyes. Luther Hooper, weaver and author of the classic book 'Hand-loom Weaving', published in 1910, considered the lease to be the most important feature in the technique of weaving.*

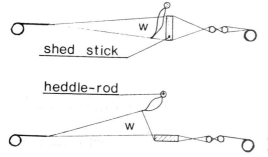

LEFT: *Inserting the weft (W) by the alternate actions of the shed stick and heddle-rod.*

*An ancient Greek pottery vessel depicting Circe's loom in a scene from Homer's 'Odyssey'. The warp is held parallel and in tension by attaching stone or pottery weights to groups of warp threads. Greek tapestries were woven using the Soumak knot, a half-hitch knot, creating an overall twill effect.*

# PRIMITIVE LOOMS

There are over six million handlooms in commercial production throughout the world and nearly all may be described as 'primitive' as they usually consist of a simple wooden frame, although the most exquisite cloth can be woven on them.

In the earliest weaving the *warp* threads were stretched parallel on a frame and darned crossways over and under with *weft* threads. Ancient tomb drawings at Beni Hasan in Egypt show simple looms with a warp held taut between two rods pegged to the ground, yet fine linen fragments reveal an astonishing 120 warp threads per centimetre (305 per inch).

It became the practice to keep alternate warp threads divided by a broad flat stick called a *shed stick*, which was turned on its edge to provide a space or *shed* through which one *pick* or length of weft thread was passed. The remaining warp threads, or *ends*, were tied with loops to a *heddle-rod*. The weaver created the first

shed by turning the shed stick and the second by pulling the heddle-rod, beating each pick down with a *sword-stick* to make cloth.

A further development was the *double-heddle*, exemplified by the Indian pit loom. Warp threads were arranged alternately through two sets of heddles suspended in a square bamboo frame. The weaver sat with his legs in a pit under the loom, controlling the heddles or *healds* with cords attached to his feet, leaving his hands free to pass the weft from side to side.

Lightweight cottons and muslins, the traditional product of the Indian pit loom, are now largely produced by a sophisticated textile industry centred in coastal towns and cities such as Bombay, although hand weaving flourishes in rural areas. Nepal has three types of weaving. Cotton weavers in southern Nepal use modern countermarche handlooms to produce 'Kathmandu' cloth in distinctive

*A young Ghanaian weaving strip cloth on a double-heddle loom. The rolled-up warp is kept on a wooden sledge behind the loom and pulled along as required. The Ashanti weavers traditionally produce narrow 'Kente' cloth, 100 to 170 millimetres (4 to 6⅝ inches) wide, which is sewn into garments or formed into a 'wrapper', a rectangular wrap-around skirt. African narrow fabric weaving can be traced back to the eleventh century and in pre-colonial days formed part of a sophisticated money system. Long lengths of cloth money were folded for market trading or wound into rolls for use when travelling. The importation of cloth ended cloth-money exchange in the late nineteenth century.*

black, green, white and apricot stripes. In central rural areas woollen cloth is produced on ground and backstrap looms; carpets are woven in the north because of the strong Tibetan influence.

Weaving in Africa is concentrated in the northern states, where as many as twelve types of primitive loom have been identified. A notable African feature is the *fixed warp,* whereby a long length of warp is tied between two points and cloth is formed by the weaver working along the warp, sometimes aided by a movable frame such as a tripod. Vertical looms predominate in Angola and Zaire and horizontal treadle looms in Nigeria and Ghana. The distinctive West African horizontal treadle loom probably found its way into Africa from Europe through the ancient trade in textiles with Saharan tribes. These looms are used by the Hausa of north Nigeria to produce narrow-strip 'turkudi' cloth, chiefly used by

the Tuaregs of the Sahara for veils and turbans.

In the Sudan Berber women weave tent strips on ground looms using a mixture of wool, goats' hair and esparto grass. Decorative textiles for bags and blankets are woven on vertical frames. The Peul of north-west Mali are renowned blanket weavers on distinctive horizontal looms with the side frames sloping towards the weaver, who uses very long pedals to operate the heald shafts.

Native weaving is no longer practised in southern Africa, although an ancient weaving culture existed in Zimbabwe and Shona migrants may have taken weaving skills as far south as northern Transvaal and Natal. The fixed-warp ground loom with single heddle-rod was common in south-east Africa and used to weave a wide cotton cloth. Some reports mention the use of a thick porridge applied as a glue to hold the warp threads in position on the warp beam.

After European settlement the rich profits achieved by importing Indian cottons made opposition to native cloth official Portuguese imperial policy. European textile manufacturers became adept at copying the style and design of African cloths so that by 1886 the British consul in Lourenco Marques reported the complete absence of native weaving and indigenous textile skills were lost for ever.

*The Navaho learned to weave from the Pueblo Indians of the Rio Grande valley, adopting their vertical blanket loom. Using a plain-weave tapestry technique, the Navaho produced large natural 'chiefs' blankets in the classic period of the early nineteenth century. These inventive weavers shredded and re-spun red English baize or 'bayeta' to provide a red yarn. The bayeta period ended in 1863 when Kit Carson confined the Navaho to the Bosque Redondo reservation. In 1868 they returned to their nomadic way of life but with the construction of the railroad brightly coloured aniline dyes were brought from Germantown, Pennsylvania, inaugurating a period of 'eye-dazzlers'. The quality of Navaho weaving declined to the point where the rugs, copies of oriental types, were sold by weight alone.*

ABOVE: *A Japanese print of a girl weaving on a backstrap loom, or 'izari-bata'. Although a reed of split bamboo is used, the weft is inserted and beaten down with a large shuttle made of oak. During the time of the shoguns stringent laws were introduced restricting artistic freedom, so traditional weaving expressed itself in quality, with every process carried out in a precise and exacting manner. Traditional craft weaving suffered with the influx of western ideas after the Meiji restoration in 1868. Japanese weavers re-equipped with Jacquard looms but within twenty years were again overwhelmed by the mass importation of powerlooms by Platt Brothers of Oldham. The izari-bata forms part of a traditional weaving system. Kasuri weaving, or ikat, involves the detailed preparation of yarn which is tied into small bundles and dyed to achieve subtle faded effects. The weaving is slow and tedious, taking several months to produce one tan of material (12 yards by 12 inches, 11 metres by 305 millimetres), enough to make one kimono.*

LEFT: *With the invention of the fly shuttle a weaver no longer had to throw the shuttle from hand to hand through the warp. A normal sley or batten was extended to incorporate shuttle boxes at either side of a flat board or shuttle race placed in front of the reed. Each shuttle box had a buffer or 'picker', which was attached to a central handle or picking peg held by the weaver. By one simple tug of the picking peg the picker struck the shuttle, propelling it through the warp to the opposite shuttle box. Drop boxes, which allow any shuttle to be brought level with the shuttle race, can also be seen on this very broad handloom made by Thomas Kennedy of Galashiels.*

6

*Before the invention of the fly shuttle a weaver had to throw the shuttle through the warp shed and was limited in the width of cloth he could weave to the distance between his outstretched arms. Broadcloths were woven by two weavers: each operated a set of treadles simultaneously and the shuttle was thrown through the warp from one weaver to the other, both pulling the heavy batten, or sley, for beat up after each throw. Shuttles were boat-shaped for ease of throwing. The boy in the foreground of this illustration from the 'Ypres Book of Trades' of 1310 is winding cops or pirns of weft thread which fit inside the shuttle.*

# PLAIN WEAVING

Vertical warp weighted looms were superseded in Europe by *horizontal looms* from about the thirteenth century. Lifting the horizontal warp threads was operated by treadles, leaving the weaver's hands free to throw the shuttle and beat up the weft, speeding up production.

Organised weaving in England was controlled by guilds in all clothmaking towns. The first craft guild, the Weavers Company of London, was established in 1100 and the Company of Blanket Weavers in Witney, Oxfordshire, as late as 1711. Until 1847 every blanket made in the town was weighed and measured for quality by officers of the 'Witney Blanketeers' under charter from Queen Anne. The famous Witney blankets were woven by family firms, notably the Colliers and

Chas Early and Marriot. The Early family, one of the oldest textile firms in Britain, continues to produce blankets.

Woollen cloth was generally woven plain, heavily fulled and dyed. Cloth production became big business — exportable cloths were taxed and Aulnagers, the King's agents, checked standards and collected taxes, stamping each piece with a lead seal.

An increase in cloth production and harsh guild restrictions led to the growth of a rural-based domestic system as weaving became a family enterprise. Weavers, usually men, also did the warping and drawing in; children carded the fleece and women spun yarn. The typical English handloom of two or four shafts was a substantial piece of equipment made of

7

solid timbers forming a four-poster framework measuring 2.5 metres by 2 metres by 2 metres high (8 feet 2 inches by 6 feet 7 inches by 6 feet 7 inches). It worked on a simple counterbalance system; as one shaft was raised the other was lowered, forming a V-shaped shed.

Country weavers were often also farmers, known as yeoman weavers, most common in Pennine regions where land was not good enough to sustain a living. They were independent weavers who bought their own wool, spun and wove it into standard cloth and took their piece to market, usually by packhorse, to towns like Huddersfield and Rochdale. A typical yeoman weaver, Cornelius Ashworth of Waltroyd near Halifax, wrote in his diary in November 1782: 'a fine frosty clear droughty day. Sized a warp and churned in the forenoon. In the afternoon wove 5 yards.'

The introduction of *new draperies* by immigrants from Europe in the late sixteenth century signalled the growth of the *putting-out* system as these new light-weight cloths using worsted, linen and cotton yarns became fashionable. Unlike wool, the supply of linen and cotton was irregular and it was necessary for merchants to buy linen from Ireland and cotton from Smyrna and put these out to weavers, paying them a fee for weaving.

Many merchants were nonconformists and as such they were from 1643 forbidden university education or entry to the professions; this was why many had turned to trade. The Gregs of Styal, Cheshire, David Whitehead of Lancashire and Thomas Fox of Wellington, Somerset, were all nonconformists who founded textile dynasties in the eighteenth century. Thomas Fox, a West of England clothier, built up a world-wide reputation for quality cloth, changing from traditional West Country broadcloth production to weaving *long ells,* a type of wool worsted serge, exported to northern China by the East India Company in exchange for huge quantities of tea.

Broadcloth production was made

*Edmund Cartwright's second powerloom of 1786 attempted to include all the basic actions of weaving as well as sizing and stop motions if either a warp or weft thread broke. Although over-complicated, it acted as a catalyst to other inventors and generated numerous variations, culminating in a successful powerloom designed by the engineer Richard Roberts of Roberts Sharpe and Company. This metal loom amalgamated successful elements of previous patents such as Vaucanson's 'perfect' cloth take-up rollers, Horrocks's crank for propelling the shuttle, and wipers or cams for heald-shaft movement.*

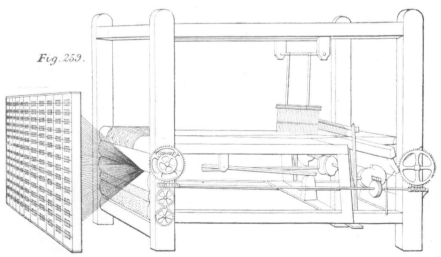

Fig. 259.

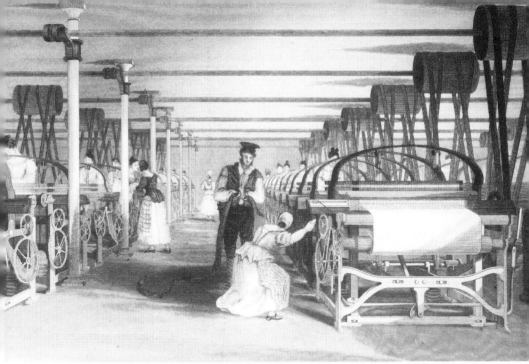

*These steam-driven powerlooms illustrated in Edward Baines's 'History of the Cotton Manufacture' copy the actions of the flying shuttle device of the handloom. A single stick under the centre of the loom, acting like a windscreen wiper, threw the shuttle from side to side. This type of picking action was quickly abandoned in favour of two sticks activated by individual cams at both sides of the loom. These centre-pick looms mark a significant stage in the development of the powerloom and early examples have been discovered in rural Wales.*

easier by the invention of the fly shuttle device in 1733 by John Kay of Bury. By sitting centrally at his loom a single weaver could propel the shuttle through the shed. Ironically, the fly shuttle device which proved so useful in broadcloth weaving was adopted against the patent rights by woollen weavers in the narrow Kersey-making areas of north Lancashire. Kay's son, Robert, helped popularise the fly shuttle by inventing a drop box mechanism in 1760, allowing shuttles of different-coloured weft to be used with the fly shuttle, extending its use to check weaving.

With the mechanisation of spinning, handloom weaving was at a premium, commanding high wages. This 'golden age' of the handloom weaver ended with an influx of unskilled labour, lowering quality and accelerating powerloom development. Edmund Cartwright's first powerloom of 1785 was one of many impractical machines patented. It took two strong men to work it and the shuttle springs had the power of a 'Congreve rocket'. Cartwright redesigned his loom in five different patents, setting up a powerloom factory in Doncaster, which failed, probably through bad management.

The major obstacle to powerloom development was the necessary application of a starch solution or *size* to cotton or woollen warp threads to give them strength during weaving. Every yard or so the weaver had to stop to size a new section of warp, drying it with hot irons. Radcliffe's *dressing frame* of 1803 solved the problem by sizing and drying the warp threads prior to winding on to the warp beam, allowing continuous weaving and rapid progress in powerloom technology.

*The Northrop loom, with its distinctive rotating battery containing refill weft pirns, was the first successful automatic loom. The automatic action relied on a mechanical feeler which touched the weft-carrying pirn through a special slit in the shuttle each time it entered the left-hand shuttle box. When there was only a small amount of yarn remaining on the pirn the feeler motion activated a lever which triggered a mechanical action on the right-hand side of the loom. As the shuttle returned to the right-hand box a powerful transfer hammer pushed a new pirn into the shuttle, ejecting the empty one through the bottom of the shuttle into a container under the loom. This automatic transfer occurred without slowing or stopping the loom.*

The powerloom was seen as the cause of much hardship for handloom weavers, especially after the Napoleonic wars when wages fell dramatically, leading to the Lancashire riots of 1826. Hundreds of handloom weavers travelled between Chadderton in the south and Clitheroe in the north, destroying powerlooms.

Despite widespread opposition powerlooms were adopted because they produced better quality cloth faster and with less skill than handlooms. Early powerlooms were known as *wiper looms* because the basic actions were controlled by rotating ovoid tappets or 'wipers'. The development of Horrocks's crank loom in 1803 separated the beat up, controlling it by a crank, leaving tappets to operate lifting of the shafts. These powerlooms were restricted to producing plain or twilled cloth, handlooms remaining the

most economical way of weaving checks, fancy patterns and broadcloths.

The most unpopular aspect of woollen handloom weaving was wetting weft cops to facilitate close packing of the weft threads. Cops of yarn were immersed in cold water and the weaver sucked water through them with a wooden tube. Transition to powerloom weaving in the woollen industry was much slower than with cotton or worsted. Woollen cloth was woven with soft spun yarns to aid the finishing process of fulling but was unsuitable for the heavy mechanical actions of early powerlooms. Woollen powerlooms of the 1850s wove at speeds of forty-eight picks per minute, little faster than a handloom, whereas worsted looms were achieving 160 picks per minute and the Harrison cotton powerloom shown at the Great Exhibition of 1851 could weave

220 picks per minute.

By the late nineteenth century the industrial revolution in textiles had created a vast system of mills producing and exporting millions of yards of cloth. A weaving shed could contain over one thousand looms, creating an astonishing and deafening noise, and weavers learnt to communicate by lip reading and sign language. Traditional looms were stopped every few minutes in order to replace the empty weft pirn or cop in the shuttle and this limited the number of looms one weaver could operate to about four.

The first successful loom to replace the weft automatically was the *Northrop*, patented by the Draper Corporation of Hopedale, Massachusetts. Ira Draper, inventor of an improved fly-shuttle hand-loom in 1816, founded loom making in a cabin called the 'Little Red Shop', which still stands beside the firm's later foundry. James Northrop, a Yorkshireman who emigrated to America and worked for the Draper Corporation, invented an automatic transfer system which replaced the weft pirns in the shuttle without slowing or stopping the loom, allowing one weaver to tend sixteen looms. The essential warp stop motion, which stopped the loom if a warp thread broke, was developed by Northrop's colleague Charles Roper. The Northrop automatic loom quickly came into use in America, coinciding with a shift of textile production from the northern states to the southern cotton-picking areas, so that by 1930 90 per cent of American looms were automatic compared with only 5 per cent in Britain.

*The common treadle loom with four or six shafts was generally limited to the production of plains, twills and satins. The jack loom was midway between the plain and the fancy loom as it could operate with as many as sixteen shafts. On a sixteen-shaft loom there were sixteen treadles; each was tied to sets of levers called lams — short lams to lower the shafts and long lams to lift shafts via the pivoted jacks on top of the loom. Only one treadle was pressed at a time to raise and lower selected shafts according to the tie-up but treadles could be operated in any order, giving capacity for a variety of weave effects or large-scale designs.*

ABOVE: *According to legend the first silk was spun in 2640 BC by the Empress Si-ling-chi and woven into a robe for her husband, Huang-to. This seventeenth-century watercolour shows a typical ancient Chinese drawloom. The drawboy on top of the loom is lifting groups of drawstrings or harness cords to raise pre-arranged numbers of threads to form a figured pattern in the cloth. This was known as 'pang hua' or 'pulling the flowers'. The fancy weave interlaced with a solid ground weave created by the weaver operating the set of heald-shafts at the front of the loom. Warp threads were passed singly through each heddle eye in the shafts and in groups of between two and ten through each eyehole or mail in the harness cords. Thus, by lifting five threads instead of one, a pattern five times larger could be woven. This arrangement, known as a 'pressure harness', allowed extremely fine silk threads to be woven in large motifs and designs.*

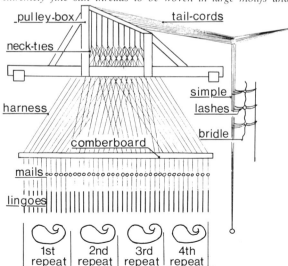

LEFT: *A front view of the European drawloom adapted from John Murphy's 'The Art of Weaving' published in 1831. In the drawloom the heald-shafts were replaced by a harness of individual cords or drawstrings held in position by a perforated board called a comberboard. Warp threads were passed in regular order through a mail fixed to each harness cord and the mass of hanging drawstrings was stabilised by attaching long thin weights, called lingoes, to the end of each cord. The lingoes restored the harness to its correct position after lifting. Complete groups of drawstrings were repeated across the width of the loom with corresponding cords in each repeat joined to a single neck-cord. The whole assembly was called a monture.*

*A membership card of the Marseilles Quilt Weavers Society, about 1825, clearly showing the action of the drawloom. The drawboy is pulling a group of simples, displacing the tail-cords and lifting the harness cords in front of the weaver. Notice the weaver using a fly-shuttle device to propel the shuttle through the warp. Marseilles quilts were coverlets of white cotton woven in complex patterns and traditionally produced in the Bolton area. Samuel Crompton of Bolton, the inventor of the spinning mule, was a weaver renowned for his exceptional skill in quilt design.*

# THE FANCY LOOM

In order to create fancy woven fabrics such as damask and brocade the weaver had to control small numbers of warp threads at will and it was probably the need to manipulate such a fine and lustrous thread as silk that led to the development of the *Chinese drawloom,* which overcame the patterning limitations of the plain loom. Two people were required to work the drawloom — a weaver and a drawboy, who sat on top of the loom raising groups of warp threads to form a pattern.

The use of the drawloom spread with the secret of silk production along the ancient 'Silk Road'. Once established in Sicily, knowledge of the drawloom travelled to Italy, where Florence and Lucca became renowned for the weaving

of exquisite figured velvets during the Renaissance. Encouraged by Louis XI of France, a colony of Italian weavers settled in Tours and later Lyons, which became the chief silk-weaving centre of Europe. Lifting on the European drawloom was controlled from the side of the loom by the drawboy and was achieved by placing a pulley box on the top frame and running a *tail-cord* from each neckcord to a fixed position on a nearby wall. Hanging from the middle of each tailcord was a vertical string known as a *simple.* Working from the design, the weaver linked groups of simples together to form *lashes* and it was the task of the drawboy to pull each lash in the correct sequence.

In general, England produced plain

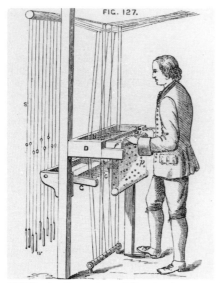

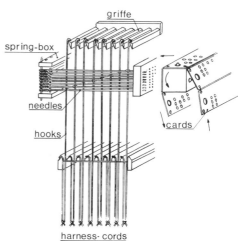

FIG. 127.

LEFT: *An illustration of Bouchon's paper-roll selection device of 1725. The operator rotated the paper roll line by line, pushing it against a set of needles acting on the simples. A hole in the paper allowed the needle to remain back while a blank pushed the simple forward into a comb-like trapboard lowered by a treadle. The fancy weaving industry has turned full circle in that most modern Jacquard and dobby looms have reverted to the use of punched paper rolls.*

RIGHT: *Essential elements of the Jacquard mechanism. The square cylinder swings away from the machine and rotates to present a new card to the machine. A hole in the pattern card allows the spring-loaded needle to remain forward, placing the hook in the path of the rising griffe, which lifts the warp threads. A blank on the pattern card pushes the needle and hook out of the path of the griffe. English coarse pitch has between one hundred and nine hundred hooks but has given way to French fine pitch, the Vincenzi and the Verdol using over fifteen hundred hooks. In theory there is no limit to the size of design which may be achieved, especially if machines are combined to increase figuring capacity. A woven picture of the Statue of Liberty was made by Barlow and Jones of Manchester using two six-hundred and two three-hundred machines, which required 22,600 cards.*

woollen cloth although fancy weaving was carried out in London and East Anglia. In 1565 the city of Norwich petitioned Queen Elizabeth I to allow Dutch and Walloon refugees to settle there. These Protestant weavers greatly revitalised its textile industry. Protestants in France obtained religious freedom from Henri IV by the Edict of Nantes but when Louis XIV revoked the Edict in 1685 many thousands of weavers from Lyons fled to England to avoid persecution. These Huguenot weavers settled mainly in the Spitalfields district of London and established a new era of prosperity in fancy weaving. They built houses with loomshops to accommodate the drawloom and rapidly became respected members of society. In 1703 Gainsborough was commissioned to paint a

portrait of Joseph Walters, 'silk manufacturer of Bow'.

In the hands of these skilled weavers the drawloom could produce beautiful cloth but had many disadvantages. Each new design took two weeks to tie up, and mistakes were easily made while pulling the lashes, especially with the increasing demand for more complex patterns. Enlarging the size of design by putting groups of threads through each harness mail resulted in a jagged effect on the curved lines in the cloth. Highly coloured work required a lash for each colour, with a group of lashes linked by a *bridle* equivalent to only one line of weft. A succession of heavy lifts made the work of the drawboy increasingly difficult. British efforts to improve the drawloom resulted in the *counterpoise harness* invented by

James Cross, which allowed one lash to rise as the other fell. A machine called a *mechanical drawboy,* a rocking cam or 'pecker' which selected the simples in turn, came into use around 1800 and enjoyed brief popularity. Developments in France, however, aimed at achieving an efficient way of selecting simples, led eventually to the invention of a fully automatic selection device.

In 1725 Basile Bouchon used a roll of paper with punched holes to indicate the required simples. Three years later Falcon substituted a chain of pattern cards on a square *cylinder* for the paper roll. Both methods allowed the drawboy to lift the harness with a treadle. In 1745 a gifted mechanic, Jacques de Vaucanson, placed the whole mechanism on top of the loom, used paper-roll selection and arranged lifting by a treadle-operated blade or *griffe.* His machine caused great unrest among French weavers and was never accepted. Joseph Marie Jacquard brought this line of development to perfection by adapting Vaucanson's selection device and incorporating Falcon's chain of pattern cards. The machine

was patented in 1801 and exhibited in Paris in 1804. However, the first Jacquards to appear in Lyons were publicly destroyed and accepted only through economic necessity some years later.

Jacquard's device was patented in England by Francis Lambert in May 1820, but it was Stephen Wilson of Lea Wilson and Company of Spitalfields who effectively introduced a working Jacquard by sending an industrial spy to Paris to discover details of the 'New French Drawloom'. In a letter dated August 1820 the spy reported he had seen the whole process including the essential punching of the pattern cards and as requested was returning with a hook and a piece of the pasteboard 'to show the texture'. This allowed Wilson to patent an improved Jacquard and card-cutting equipment enabling him to manufacture machines for his fellow weavers.

The Jacquard mechanism removed the need for a drawboy and could control individual warp threads, giving greater definition of outline to curved patterns. Designs could be changed within minutes and pattern cards stored for future use. It

*The firm of Cartwright and Sheldon operated in Macclesfield as silk cloth manufacturers until 1981, when the business was sold. Their unique collection of twenty-eight Jacquard handlooms in Lower Paradise Mill has been preserved and forms part of a Silk Heritage Museum. Silk production was started in Macclesfield by Charles Roe in 1743 following the decline of the button-making industry and new skills were introduced by Huguenot weavers secretly brought to Macclesfield by Leigh and Voce in 1790. Jacquard looms were used in houses as well as factories, and many houses in the town still retain their roof-top workshops. Powerlooms came into use after 1830 with most manufacturers specialising in ties and silk pictures. These woven pictures, usually measuring 230 by 120 millimetres (9 by 4¾ inches), were called 'Stevengraphs' after Thomas Stevens of Coventry.*

was operated by a single treadle, making it suitable for the eventual application of power and the extra height and expense of the Jacquard loom caused a steady movement towards loomshop and factory use. By the mid nineteenth century Jacquards were in operation throughout Britain. In London the Jacquard superseded the drawloom for weaving fine silks; in Coventry and Nuneaton it was used for ribbon manufacture and in Macclesfield for shawls and ties. Henry Tootal of Manchester bought Jacquard handlooms to produce silk handkerchiefs and around 1840 installed Jacquard powerlooms in a factory where one man could attend two looms. Jacquard weaving of linen damask took place in remote cottages in Ireland until the early twentieth century, when the craft became centralised in factories.

Fancy weaving was established in Paisley near Glasgow in 1760 as an offshoot of the Spitalfields trade but the town rapidly developed a distinctive style, specialising in the production of shawls incorporating the familiar 'pine' motif derived from the shape of the mango fruit. Paisley shawls were woven versions of embroidered Indian Cashmere shawls and utilised botany wool warp and silk weft. They were woven face down on the loom to avoid a succession of heavy lifts and as they were highly coloured up to ten shuttle boxes were used. The Jacquard device allowed intricate reversible designs to be introduced but the Jacquard powerloom led to the decline of the shawl. Once a valued traditional wedding gift, the powerloom cheapened the shawl and production ceased in the 1870s when Paisley shawls became unfashionable. During the slump many Paisley weavers emigrated to Paterson, New Jersey, the silk town of the United States of America.

Jacquards were enthusiastically adopted in Halifax for weaving cotton and worsted damasks but not in Huddersfield, where the *witch* adequately produced small decorative motifs on waistcoat material. The *Leeds Mercury* reported in 1829 that the fancy trade in Huddersfield had been 'considerably revived by the introduction of a machine called a Witch which enables the weaver to beautify the cloth with a great variety of flowers'. This device, operated by a single treadle, was originally termed a *drum witch*, a rotating wooden drum or

*A dobby selection device made by George Wood, showing the cylinder and pattern chain of lags and pegs. Each lag represents one shoot of weft and pegs are inserted to denote shaft lifts. A peg deflects a hook, which is directly linked to a heald shaft, into the path of a rising blade. Groups of shafts are usually lifted to form a pre-arranged pattern. After each weft insertion the cylinder is rotated, presenting the next lag to the row of hooks. The origins of the dobby are obscure although a patent of 1824 by John Potter described an early form of dobby known as a 'drum witch'.*

*Many Spitalfields weavers moved out of London in the nineteenth century and established workshops in Essex and East Anglia. Stephen Walters, a weaver of Huguenot descent, moved to Sudbury in Suffolk and the firm continues to weave silk. His brother Daniel acquired Pound End Mill in Braintree, built by Samuel Courtauld in 1818, and installed over 150 Jacquard looms. In 1893 the firm was taken over by Warner and Sons and under Sir Frank Warner became world-famous for producing rich furnishing silks. Warner and Sons gave up weaving in 1971 but the Spitalfields tradition of handloom weaving was carried on by Richard Humphries, the last trainee designer with Warners, who acquired a collection of the looms in order to establish his own weaving company at De Vere Mill, Castle Hedingham, in Essex. In this photograph Mr Peter Gowers of Humphries Weaving Company is weaving a pure silk damask containing nearly twenty thousand warp threads.*

barrel studded with pegs acting directly on hooks to lift groups of heald-shafts. Knowledge of the Jacquard card chain prompted a more refined version known as the *dobby* using a chain of wooden bars or *lags* containing pegs to control lifting. The new machines coincided with a fashion for 'fancy trowsering' and led the firm of Gill and Sugden to establish a mill to make fancy cloth using Jacquards. It was so successful that other prominent manufacturers followed their example. John Brooke and Sons of Honley, who had been weaving in Huddersfield since the sixteenth century, bought two Jacquard powerlooms in 1842, another eight in 1852 and twenty more in 1854, reflecting the rapid increase in fancy cloth production.

Initially Jacquard and dobby powerlooms were less efficient than handlooms but the introduction of the double-lift Jacquard with rising and falling griffes allowed fast production and in 1867 Hattersley and Smith patented a double-lift dobby, leading to a proliferation of dobby looms throughout West Yorkshire and the fancy cotton weaving area of Nelson and Colne in Lancashire. The combination of fashion, technical innovation and a generation of brilliant designers established Yorkshire as the premier producer of low-cost fancy woollens and high-quality worsted, causing a sharp decline in the West of England textile industry.

The Edwardian era saw the greatest expression of Jacquard weaving as highly ornamental Art Nouveau designs became universally fashionable. Since 1920 there has been a severe contraction of fancy weaving in Britain although technical development of the dobby and Jacquard has continued. The introduction of artificial silk and man-made fibres undermined the established silk industry. English coarse pitch Jacquards with six needles per square centimetre (thirty-nine per square inch) have given way to the French fine pitch system, particularly the *Verdol*, a compact versatile device using twenty needles per square centimetre (129 per square inch). General acceptance of the Verdol has allowed the production of large patterns without the use of a pressure harness. The Jacquard head is now supported on a gantry above the loom, allowing access for cleaning and repairing, and dobby mechanisms once manufactured as part of the loom are now separate, often positioned on the floor adjacent to the loom. Both selection devices use punched paper rolls and may be electronically operated. Most traditional dobby looms have been replaced by flexible rapier and shuttleless looms using Staubli dobbies.

The modern industry now uses computer Jacquards which can scan a design and transfer it immediately to fabric, electronically, without the need for paper rolls.

LEFT: *Industrial belting looms made by Robert Hall and Son of Bury, now preserved in a unique mill museum in Gothenburg, Sweden.*
BELOW: *Lappet fabric consists of extra warp or 'whip' threads stitched into a fine ground cloth woven face down on the loom. The wheel at the side of the loom has one tooth for every pick of weft and the internal contours operate needle bars in a side-to-side pattern movement. Lappet looms produce traditional Indian and Islamic dress goods such as yashmaks and keffiyehs.*

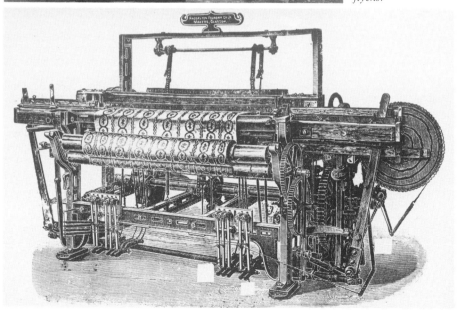

*A four man chenille handloom. 'Chenille', from the French for caterpillar, is a furry yarn made by cutting up lengths of specially woven cloth and was used to give a pile surface to a flat-woven carpet or upholstery cloth. This technique was developed by James Templeton of Glasgow in the 1840s.*

# CARPETS AND SPECIAL EFFECTS

An important sector in British textiles has been the production of speciality fabrics. By the late nineteenth century Britain could produce almost any type of fabric by machine and dominated production of such diverse materials as cotton saris, industrial belting and woven carpets.

The arrival of oriental carpets in the west during the sixteenth century excited great admiration but their expense caused the French king Henri IV to instruct Pierre Dupont to establish a workshop, or atelier, to produce 'French orientals'. Under Louis XIII Dupont created a second workshop outside Paris, appointing Simon Lourdet as director. They converted a children's home, called the Hospice de la Savonnerie, built on the site of a former soap factory, and their carpets with floral designs in baroque and rococo styles became known as *Savonneries*. A flat tapestry-style carpet was produced at the Aubusson atelier.

In England, a flat-woven floor covering called *fote-cloth* was made on broadlooms with coarse wools unsuitable for clothing, and in Kidderminster around 1745 Pearsall and Broom developed a patterned flat-weave rug known as *Kidder*, later called Scotch or Ingrain carpet. Henry Herbert, ninth Earl of Pembroke, toured Europe in 1740 and saw the production of vertical-warp Savonneries and Brussels loop-pile carpets on horizontal looms. He was so impressed that he started a carpet-weaving factory at his country house at Wilton in Wiltshire.

The weavers of Kidder carpets soon realised they could not compete with Brussels loop-pile so John Broom journeyed to Flanders, returning with a master weaver, who constructed carpet looms for Kidderminster, making the standard carpet width 68 centimetres (27 inches), a Flemish ell.

Brussels and Wilton carpets were woven with a linen ground warp and a coloured pile warp held in frames behind the loom. These worsted yarns were drawn down during weaving according to the pattern. Only one row of loops appeared on the surface at any one time; the others were hidden in the body of the carpet, making it a very expensive product. Brussels loops were formed by the insertion of round wires and Wiltons by

*The Skinner and Smith tufting loom, shown here at the London Exhibition of 1862, was the forerunner of the spool Axminster. It was devised by Halcyon Skinner, who worked for Alexander Smith of Yonkers, New York, and was designed to create highly decorative pile carpets. Any number of colours could be incorporated into the carpet as each spool was wound with a variety of coloured yarns to form one row of tufts in the pattern. The ground weave was created by two weft threads interweaving with the warp. Pile was inserted from one spool at a time, the ends of the pile yarn being drawn into the carpet, turned up into a V shape and cut from the spool, which moved away on a conveyor system as the next spool carrying another set of pile threads came into operation. Michael Tomkinson bought the patent rights in 1872 and renamed the loom the Royal Axminster, describing it as 'the manufacturer's dream'. The impressive conveyor system, sometimes extending through five floors of a mill, carried a large number of spools operating successively, one complete rotation being equal to one pattern repeat.*

oval wires, producing a longer pile, which was cut to give a velvet-type carpet. The ground warp was on two levels, the *chain* actively combining the weft and pile, while the *stuffer* warp acted as a filler and base for the loops. Brussels had two and Wilton three weft threads to every row of pile.

Thomas Whitty of Axminster, attempting to imitate oriental or 'Turkey' carpets, visited a weaving workshop in Fulham operated by Peter Parisot and other French immigrants. He decided to copy their vertical loom technique and 'on midsummer day 1755 . . . I begun the first carpet I ever made taking my children with their Aunt Betty Harvey to overlook and assist them for my first workers.' These hand-knotted *Axminsters* became famous and production continued until 1835, when their manufacture was transferred to Wilton.

The Kidderminster carpet trade flourished, especially after the arrival of jute from Bengal and the introduction of the Jacquard by Lea and Broom in 1828, but lost its position to Halifax when it failed to adopt processes for producing cheaper carpets. Richard Whytock of Edinburgh in 1832 devised a method of producing multi-coloured carpets cheaply, with all the expensive wool on the surface. In the Whytock tapestry technique a complete carpet warp was wound around a large drum and the threads coloured according to the pattern but elongated to allow for the rising pile during weaving. Whytock started production, converting the old St Ann's brewery in 1833, and his idea was immensely successful, drastically reducing the output of Brussels carpets.

A Brussels powerloom, invented by Erastus Bigelow of Massachusetts, was shown at the Great Exhibition and at Hoobrook Mill in Kidderminster but was rejected by local manufacturers. Crossleys of Halifax immediately bought the patent rights. John Crossley established carpet production at Dean Clough, Halifax, in 1803 and expanded rapidly after taking a franchise to produce Whytock's tapestry carpets. By acquiring Bigelow's powerloom patent Crossleys dominated carpet production for many years, becoming the largest producer of carpets in the world.

The challenge of mechanically reproducing the Axminster technique was realised by Halcyon Skinner and it appeared in Britain as the *Royal Axminster*. Development of *spool* and *gripper* Axminster powerlooms revitalised Kidderminster, which is again the leading centre of carpet production in Britain. Weaving two carpets at once by the face-to-face or *double-plush* method was introduced in the 1920s, increasing the cost-effectiveness of woven carpets. Recently, woven carpet manufacture has declined in favour of non-woven tufted carpets with latex or rubberised backings.

*John Brinton, whose family had been carpet weavers in Kidderminster since 1770, purchased a gripper device from Halcyon Skinner in 1885 and had to build a complete gripper Axminster loom to go with it. The beak-like gripper took a tuft of yarn from frames behind the loom and positioned it in the warp, where a weft thread secured it. A gripper-spool loom combining the best of both Axminster techniques was developed in the 1930s by David Crabtree and Sons. This is an Axminster eight-frame gripper loom.*

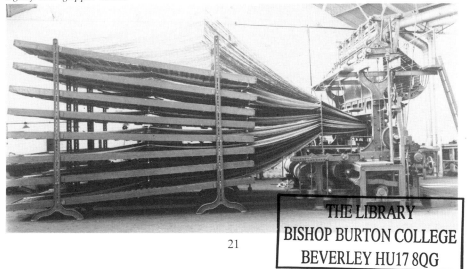

21

LEFT: *Ribbon, tape or smallwares manufacture is a little known branch of the weaving trade. Narrow fabrics were originally woven on ordinary handlooms until William Dircxz of Sonnevelt in Holland invented the Dutch Engine loom in 1603, for weaving twelve pieces at a time. A patent of 1745 by John Kay and John Stell describes the application of power to the Dutch Engine loom by 'sundry tappits which tread the necessary treadles and move the batten or lath.' In the mid eighteenth century Vaucanson replaced shuttle throwing pegs or drivers with a rack and pinion which gave positive action to D-shaped shuttles carrying bobbins or quills. This method is still in use on these modern Muller Jacquard looms weaving labels.*

RIGHT: *This terry-towel loom has two back beams, one for the ground and an extra beam on a different tension for the loops which are formed by a special reed action. A cam holds the reed back from the fell of the cloth for two picks of weft but on the third pick it is allowed forward, pushing the pile warp into loops above and below the ground weave. The towel pattern is created on the loom by a cross border dobby, which has two pattern chain cylinders, plus an intermediate which allows transfer from one to the other, enabling squared designs, mixtures of plain and loop weave, and fancy patterns to be woven.*

RIGHT: *This speciality loom produces leno or gauze fabrics. Shafts at the front of the loom, called 'doup-healds', contain special heald wires which cross chosen warp threads, forming an open cellular structure. The leno structure is particularly safe and warm for use as cot or pram blankets.*

BELOW: *Nineteenth-century fustian looms in Nutclough Mill, Hebden Bridge, West Yorkshire, a former centre of fustian weaving. Fustians, said to originate from El Fustada near Cairo, are heavy weft pile cottons which are woven with a large number of weft threads. These are later cut and brushed into ribs of pile, forming corduroy, or simply raised and cropped to produce moleskin. Hard-wearing traditional fustians are still woven at Cudworths of Norden, near Rochdale.*

ABOVE LEFT: *Ethel Coomaraswamy, later Ethel Mairet, weaving in the Norman chapel at Broad Campden, Gloucestershire, about 1910.*

ABOVE RIGHT: *The Dovecot Tapestry Studios, Edinburgh, were established in 1912 by the fourth Marquess of Bute. Two master weavers from William Morris's workshop introduced the technique of creating woven pictures on vertical or haute-lisse looms. After 1940, renamed the Edinburgh Tapestry Company, they produced new tapestries based on cartoons by Henry Moore and Graham Sutherland. Additional looms, reputedly from the famous Soho workshops and dating from 1698, were acquired at this time. Archie Brennan became artistic director in 1963 and inaugurated a dynamic revival in tapestry, based on interpretations of the work of artists such as David Hockney and Eduardo Paolozzi.*

LEFT: *A pencil sketch by Edward Burne-Jones of William Morris at the loom.*

*Between 1910 and 1930 Luther Hooper operated a weaving studio in Hammersmith and designed a shaft drawloom for his pupil Alice Hindson. This compact loom has four ground shafts and twenty-four figuring shafts, enabling extremely ornate cloth to be woven. The lashes, which can be seen at the front of the loom, indicate the required succession of lifts, with shaft lifting operated by the double-handled drawbar. Various sizes of this loom were made by different loom makers. This example is Alice Hindson's 'designer's drawloom', made by Eric Sharpe and now used by the weaver and designer Enid Russ in her studio.*

# CRAFT REVIVAL

The Great Exhibition of 1851 reflected the euphoria and confidence people felt about the machine age, but a significant group was critical of industrialisation, feeling that individual creativity had been destroyed and the quality of life reduced for most people.

The critic John Ruskin expressed this reaction in a series of essays based on his passion for Gothic architecture and medieval craftsmanship. In *Stones of Venice* Ruskin demanded a return to individuality, insisting that products of applied art should reveal their man-made origins. The chapter 'Of the nature of Gothic' greatly influenced William Morris and his friend Edward Burne-Jones. In alliance with the Pre-Raphaelite Brotherhood, a group of artists dedicated to the medieval ideal, Morris sought to regenerate art and re-create the skills and practices inherent in the medieval guilds and to develop decorative crafts as a commercial venture.

The firm of Morris, Marshall, Faulkner and Company, Fine Art Workmen, was formed in 1861 to produce a wide variety of craft objects of high quality. Morris was an enthusiastic weaver, especially of tapestry. His designs overflow with foliage, leaving little background to interfere with the prominent natural motifs. Carpet-weaving frames were established in Hammersmith and a tapestry factory opened at Merton Abbey. M Bazin from Lyons, assisted by a retired Spitalfields weaver, in 1877 set up a Jacquard loom for Morris, which was used to produce heavy woollen furnishing fabrics.

Morris and his friends inaugurated the Arts and Crafts Movement but they failed to re-create their ideal. Instead they produced an aristocracy of artists hostile to the machine age who created exquisite pieces of work. The irony for Morris was to see the population enjoy his textiles only when they were mass-produced by machines. Many fabrics, notably Morris's Dove and Rose designs, were woven by Alexander Morton of Darvel, Strathclyde, who by the age of twenty-eight employed over four hundred domestic handloom weavers.

A succession of imitators followed Morris, such as Mackmurdo's Century Guild and the Arts and Crafts Exhibition Society, founded by Walter Crane in 1888. In the same year Charles Robert Ashbee formed the Guild of Handicraft, moving to Chipping Campden, Gloucestershire, in 1902, to create a rural crafts community. In the early twentieth century Vanessa Bell designed Jacquard fabrics for the Omega Workshops; tapestry weaving was carried out by the Peasant Arts Society and linen weaving flourished in Haslemere, Surrey, using looms made by a cabinet-maker, D. D. Dolloway. Furnishing fabrics were handwoven by Edmund and Nero Hunter of the St Edmondsbury Weavers, Letchworth, Hertfordshire.

The skills of hand weaving had to be rediscovered and this pioneering spirit was typified by Ethel Mairet and Elizabeth Peacock. A weaving workshop operating an apprentice system in the Morris tradition was established in 1920 by Ethel Mairet at her house, Gospels, in Ditchling, East Sussex, using natural yarns and vegetable dyes to produce colourful primitive-style fabrics of high quality. Dolloway looms were introduced, and some technical skills brought to the workshop by Valentine KilBride, who had used looms designed by Luther Hooper and was well acquainted with the loom makers George and John Maxwell of Burgess Hill, West Sussex.

Elizabeth Peacock established a workshop called Weavers nearby and with Mabel Dawson founded the Guild of Weavers, Spinners and Dyers, achieving fame for the woven banners in the Great Hall at Dartington, Devon, designed to absorb sound and make the hall acoustically suitable for music. In addition to the ordinary four-shaft counterbalance looms, a very large loom described as a 'thirty-eight shaft drawloom' was made for Weavers by George Maxwell. Cloth lengths with extra warp patterning were woven on this drawloom by Alice Hindson and Elizabeth Peacock.

*This loom was made by George Wood, the most renowned handloom builder of the twentieth century, working in the tradition of Kennedy of Galashiels and the Maxwells of Burgess Hill. George Wood makes clocks and musical instruments as well as looms. Each part of the loom is hand-made to the highest standard and some parts, such as the breast beam, are brought to a hard finish by repeated burnishing with wood shavings. Traditional Latvian cloth is being woven on this dobby loom by the weaver and designer Rasma Budins.*

*The sturdy Harris four-shaft table loom is the ideal beginner's loom. Harris Looms was established in 1938 by Dr. C. W. Harris of Cranbrook, Kent, who built looms for occupational therapy and home weaving. It was continued in the 1950s by the Davies family of Hawkhurst,, who expanded the range of looms, incorporated the loom makers Douglas Andrew of Canterbury and acquired the rights to make the Maxwell countermarche floor loom. Harris looms are now made at Ashford in Kent by Emmerich Berlon.*

A second phase in Ethel Mairet's career made her one of the most influential weavers of the twentieth century. While visiting Denmark she met Elsa Gullberg, a weaver-designer who wove prototypes for industry. This style of work was adopted at Gospels and the apprentice system was extended to include technically advanced students from Europe experimenting with new weaves and yarns. Eight-shaft looms by Lervad were bought from Denmark and Bianca Wassmuth introduced the technique of tying up the shafts and treadles for particular weaves. Marianne Straub and Leonora Mass introduced gauze and leno weave structures using lurex and cellophane yarns. After the Second World War Ethel Mairet reverted to earlier simpler techniques but still accepted and influenced pupils such as Mary Barker and Peter Collingwood.

In Germany the architect Walter Gropius merged two Saxon schools of art in 1919 to create the *Bauhaus,* using a curriculum based on the medieval artisan system, each student having two teachers, a craftsman and an artist. The Bauhaus subsequently moved to Dessau, developing a new philosophy committed to the idea of designing for mass production.

The Exposition des Arts Decoratifs,

held in Paris in 1925, inaugurated a new style called *Art Deco,* which caused a revolution in European design. Woven textiles based on abstract and cubist forms were introduced, with great emphasis on fancy yarn effects. The artist Rodier experimented with goats' hair and wool mixtures, producing couture fabrics.

The Paris exhibition shook British designers into action, creating a fresh innovative style. Once again it was acceptable for artists to design for industry. Marion Dorn and E. McKnight Kauffer held an exhibition in 1929 displaying a range of hand-knotted rugs in jazz-age designs made by the Royal Wilton carpet factory. Their exciting ideas inspired other *modern movement* designers to explore abstract theories but the floral tradition was never completely abandoned and the commercial textile industry was happy to revert to weaving traditional designs.

Some people stand out: Marianne Straub designed upholstery cloths for Gordon Russell and worked for Warners and for Helios Limited, a branch of Barlow and Jones of Bolton. Alec Hunter, son of Edmund Hunter, produced hand-woven prototypes for powerlooms in natural, rayon and metallic yarns at Warners of Braintree. Sir James Morton,

*The Ahrens and Violette dobby loom, developed in the United States, incorporates many useful features. A side-mounted dobby selection device does not require extra headroom and enables the loom to be used by home weavers as well as professional designers. Like most American handlooms it is fitted with a sectional back beam, allowing the warp threads to be wound on in convenient narrow sections. The standard sixteen-shaft dobby may be fitted with either a lag and peg or a compu-dobby. The AVL dobby is being introduced to the Manipuri tribe of north-east Bangladesh by the Intermediate Technology Development Group. This rural tribe traditionally use a backstrap loom (jong) and a bamboo floor loom (jonghum) to produce fabrics to supplement basic farming, and it is hoped the new looms will greatly increase productivity.*

and then Alistair Morton, successfully combined art and industry, producing exciting new designs for Morton Sundour Fabrics, operating Edinburgh Weavers as an experimental workshop, aiming to create 'new forms of expression in design and texture for the modern world'.

Gordon Russell established the Design Panel to control the wartime *Utility* design and manufacturing scheme. One of the designers was Enid Marx. Essentially a fabric printer, Enid Marx had designed moquettes for the London Passenger Transport Board in the 1930s. Her Utility fabrics displayed a superb design sense even though restricted to two yarns, four colours and small repeats of pattern.

Since 1946, in contrast to a declining textile industry, interest in the craft of weaving has grown enormously and gifted textile designers have produced craft-based designs. Bernat Klein fabrics combined glowing colour and fancy yarn effects. Jack Lenor Larsen gained a worldwide reputation for his experimental textiles when he produced twenty-two silk hangings for the Sears Tower in Chicago. Looms for the amateur enthusiast have appeared, made by Harris, Dryad and Weavemaster.

The loom itself has become an object of artistic beauty and many craft weavers now describe themselves as artist-craftsmen, using the medium of weaving to create an art form. Some weavers such as Dora Jung, Irene Waller and Theo Moorman, have become fine art weavers, creating sculptural forms in textiles.

The Crafts Advisory Committee, later the Crafts Council, was established in 1971, reflecting the growing importance of crafts in society. Some craftsmen in textiles have moved again towards functional weaving but controversy remains over an acceptable definition of what characterises an artist-craftsman and the relationship of the craft weaver to industry remains largely unresolved.

*A weaving shed operating Sulzer projectile looms. Weft insertion is by a series of gripper shuttles or projectiles (90 millimetres, 3½ inches, long), which are returned to the firing position by a conveyor under the loom. A projectile grips the weft yarn and is then fired like a bullet by the action of a torsion rod which is twisted to a state of tension and released at the appropriate moment. The immense energy imparted results in rapid weft insertion.*

# WEAVING MACHINES

The automatic loom was steadily accepted so that by 1946 nearly all North American looms and one third of all powerlooms in the world had automatic weft replenishment. Inroads by the automatic system caused British loom manufacturers to make uncomfortable attempts to improve loom efficiency. Butterworth and Dickenson of Burnley made a shuttle-changing loom and a four-colour pirn-changing Dobcross was developed by Hutchinson Hollingsworth. Platt Brothers of Oldham bought automatic loom patents from Toyoda of Japan, who used this money to start the Toyota Car Company. Despite these efforts, continental looms made by Ruti, Saurer and Jaeggli, with precision dobbies by Staubli, appeared in Britain.

Many manufacturers adopted the *Unifil* system made by the Leesona Corporation of Warwick, Rhode Island. The Unifil device was attached to traditional looms and rewound empty pirns on a conveyor system. Loom developments were aimed at replacing the large noisy shuttle with other systems and it was the revolutionary *projectile* loom, developed by Sulzer Brothers of Switzerland, which inaugurated the age of the weaving machine. Although invented in 1924, the Sulzer did not appear commercially until 1953. This loom fires a small bullet-like gripper at high speed, taking weft yarn across the loom. The Sulzer has proved extremely efficient, with over twenty models developed to accommodate a variety of fabrics.

The concept of a *rapier* powerloom appeared in de Gennes' patent of 1678 and embodies the idea of transferring weft on the tip of a sword-like rapier. From 1905 to 1974 rapier looms were used at the Ripley Manufacturing Company, in Derbyshire. These traditional machines, still in use at Castle Cary in Somerset, used a single rigid rapier arm to insert strands of horsehair into a cotton warp to produce 'haircloth' for use as garment interlining. In 1932 Walter

*A Staubli dobby on a modern weaving machine. This dobby creates the weave using a paper roll punched with holes to indicate the pattern or can be directly activated by a computer-aided design system (CAD).*

Gledhill of Holmfirth, West Yorkshire, made rapier looms for the woollen trade but without success. The modern rapier loom was developed by Dornier at Landau, Germany, and launched at the 1963 International Textile Machinery Exhibition. The first machines had rigid arms which extended out of the sides of the loom, replaced later by flexible rapiers.

A loom developed by Harrison of Blackburn in the 1860s used compressed air to push the shuttle through the warp shed 'without noise and with a celerity that effectually answered the purpose'. This method proved too expensive but the idea of weft insertion by an *air jet* was put forward by Brooks of Accrington in 1911 and a corresponding suction nozzle was patented in 1929. Neither was used in practical installations but they were the

*The actions of the multi-phase loom. The warp opens at one side to allow entry of a weft-carrier or bobbin carrying enough yarn for one insertion and closes again as the bobbin travels along, with beating up taking place behind it by a rotating reed made up of contoured discs. The warp immediately opens again to allow successive weft carriers to enter until waves of warp flow across the loom. Multi-phase machines, flat and circular, achieve extremely high insertion rates. The weft is quietly inserted at a steady speed with no sudden acceleration, avoiding the peak stress of opening a complete warp.*

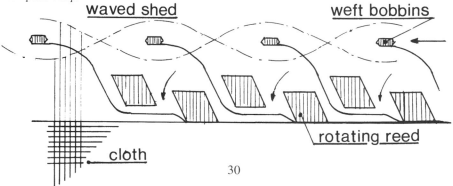

*Breaking traditional looms for scrap. In the post-war period successive governments supported a scrapping policy and paid a cash premium for each loom scrapped as an incentive for modernisation. This had the effect of diminishing specialist work in favour of the standardised, highly productive automatic system.*

forerunners of the first commercial air-jet loom, based on developments by Max Paabo of Sweden and introduced in the 1950s as the *Maxbo*. The first models blew the weft thread through the warp, initially at four hundred picks per minute. With air-jet insertion, the shed could be very narrow, placing minimum stress on the warp and allowing high speeds with less noise.

The Swiss machinery makers Ruti, using patents by Te Strake, made great advances in air-jet technology. Weft insertion rates (WIR) have been increased from 600 metres (1970 feet) to over 1000 metres (3280 feet) per minute by using relay nozzles. Maschinenfabrik Ruti amalgamated with Sulzer Brothers to develop the air-jet loom further. Jet looms using a drop of water for weft transfer were also developed but have limitations in terms of product and performance.

Although technically advanced, with computers capable of controlling most techniques of weaving, shuttleless looms still copy the actions of the medieval handloom. In the 1970s, textile research centred on the concept of a *multi-phase* loom, in which all the actions of weaving take place simultaneously, and by the early 1990s Sulzer manufactured a *Linear Wave Loom* operating at 2500 metres per minute WIR. Some technologists predict future machines could be 8 metres wide and achieve insertion rates of 5000 metres per minute WIR.

# FURTHER READING

Barlow, Alfred. *The History and Principles of Weaving by Hand and Power.* Sampson Low, Marston, Searle and Rivington, 1878.
Broudy, Eric. *The Book of Looms.* Studio Vista, 1979.
Coatts, Margot. *A Weaver's Life: Ethel Mairet.* Crafts Council, 1983.
Crossland, A. *Modern Carpet Manufacture.* Columbine Press, 1958.
Hooper, Luther. *Hand-loom Weaving.* Pitman, 1910.
Parry, Linda. *William Morris Textiles.* Crescent Books, 1995.
Timmins, Geoffrey. *Four Centuries of Lancashire Cotton.* Lancashire County Books, 1996.
Vincent, J. J. *Shuttleless Looms.* Textile Institute, 1980.

# PLACES TO VISIT

UNITED KINGDOM
*American Museum in Britain*, Claverton Manor, Bath BA2 7BD. Telephone: 01225 460503. Website: www.americanmuseum.org
*Bradford Industrial Museum and Horses at Work Museum*, Moorside Road, Eccleshill, Bradford, West Yorkshire BD2 3HP. Telephone: 01274 631756. Website: www.bradford.gov.uk/tourism/museums
*Braintree District Museum*, Manor Street, Braintree, Essex CM7 3HW. Telephone: 01376 325666. Website: www.braintree.gov.uk
*Coldharbour Mill Working Wool Museum*, Coldharbour Mill, Uffculme, Cullompton, Devon EX15 3EE. Telephone: 01884 840960. Website: www.coldharbourmill.org.uk
*Helmshore Textile Museums*, Holcombe Road, Helmshore, Rossendale, Lancashire BB4 4NP. Telephone: 01706 226459. Website: www.lancashire.gov.uk
*Macclesfield Silk Museum*, Heritage Centre, Roe Street, Macclesfield, Cheshire SK11 6UT. Telephone: 01625 613210. Website: www.silk-macclesfield.org
*Museum of Science and Industry in Manchester*, Liverpool Road, Castlefield, Manchester M3 4FP. Telephone: 0161 832 2244 or 0161 832 1830 (infoline). Website: www.msim.org.uk
*Newtown Textile Museum*, 5–7 Commercial Street, Newtown, Powys SY16 2BL. Telephone: 01686 622024.
*Paisley Museum and Art Galleries*, High Street, Paisley, Renfrewshire PA1 2BA. Telephone: 0141 889 3151.
*Paradise Mill*, Park Lane, Macclesfield, Cheshire SK11 6TJ. Telephone: 01625 618228. Website: www.silk-macclesfield.org
*Quarry Bank Mill*, Styal, Wilmslow, Cheshire SK9 4LA. Telephone: 01625 527468. Website: www.quarrybankmill.org.uk
*Queen Street Mill*, Queen Street, Harle Syke, Burnley, Lancashire BB10 2HX. Telephone: 01282 412555. Website: www.lancashire.gov.uk
*Saddleworth Museum and Art Gallery*, High Street, Uppermill, Oldham, Lancashire OL3 6HS. Telephone: 01457 874093.
*Science Museum*, Exhibition Road, South Kensington, London SW7 2DD. Telephone: 0870 870 4771. Website: www.sciencemuseum.org.uk
*Ulster Folk and Transport Museum*, Cultra Manor, Holywood, County Down BT18 0EU. Telephone: 028 9042 8428. Website: www.nidex.com/uftm

OTHER COUNTRIES
*American Textile History Museum*, 491 Dutton Street, Lowell, Massachusetts 01854, USA.
*The Colonial Williamsburg Foundation*, PO Box 1776, Williamsburg, Virginia 23187 1776. Website: www.colonialwilliamsburg.org
*Göteborgs Remfabrik*, 23 K V Bleket Tomt, Nr 5 Göteborg (Gothenburg), Sweden.
*Lorenzo Rubelli and Figlio*, San Marco 3877, Venice, Italy.
*Maison des Canuts*, 12 rue d'Ivry, 69001 Lyons, Rhône, France.
*Museum for Textiles*, 55 Centre Avenue, Toronto, Ontario, Canada M5G 2H5.
*Nederlands Textielmuseum*, Goirkestraat 96, 5046 GN Tilburg, Netherlands.
*Städtisches Museum*, Schloss Rheyt, Mönchengladbach, Germany.
*Textile Museum*, 2320 South Street, Northwest, Washington DC 20008.

ACKNOWLEDGEMENTS
Illustrations on the following pages are acknowledged to: Ashmolean Museum, Oxford, 3; Belwoven Ltd, 22 (upper); Bolton Museums and Art Gallery, 13; Bower Roebuck Ltd, 17; Brintons Carpets, 21; Carpets International UK, 19; City of Manchester, Cultural Services, 11; Crafts Study Centre, Bath, 24 (upper left); Edinburgh Tapestry Company, 24 (upper right); Emmerich (Berlon) Ltd, 27; Göteborgs Remfabrik, 18 (upper); Humphries Weaving Company, 17; *Illustrated London News*, Picture Library, 20; Intermediate Technology Development Group, 4; Lancashire County Museum, 23 (upper); A. and V. Looms, Macclesfield, 28; Macclesfield Silk Museum, Paradise Mill, 15; William Morris Gallery, Walthamstow, London, 24 (lower); Museum of New Mexico, Ben Wittick Collection, 5; Rochdale Libraries, Local Studies Collection, 1; Science Museum, London, 10; J. and M. Sherry, 22 (lower); Sulzer UK Ltd, 29; Victoria and Albert Museum, London, 12 (upper).

# EFFECTIVE SCHOOL MANAGEMENT

**Bertie Everard** read chemistry at Oxford and joined ICI in 1951 as a research chemist. He moved from the technical side in mid-career and became the Company Education and Training Manager, responsible for senior management training. Shortly before retirement in 1982 he was appointed a Visiting Professor at the Polytechnic of Central London and later a Visiting Fellow at the University of London Institute of Education, where he helped to design and run courses in school management. He undertook a year's research into the problems of school management, comparing them with those in industry, and publishing the results in another book, *Developing Management in Schools*. Recently he has been a consultant in the management of change to a project concerned with the 1981 Education Act, and helped to write the training manual, *Decision Making for Special Educational Needs*.

**Geoffrey Morris** is the managing Director of EMAS Business Consultants Ltd. Before joining EMAS (European Management Advisory Services) in 1971, he was a Senior Manager in the Unilever Group, and prior to that he was a schoolteacher for 10 years, 5 of them as Head of Modern Languages and General Studies.

In 1967 he obtained the backing of the CBI to run a course in management for schoolteachers – the first of its kind. Since then he has been active in promoting management in schools through courses at Brighton Polytechnic and Brunel University; with lectures and workshops for groups of inspectors, headteachers and administrators and consultancy and development activities within individual schools. From 1983 to 1986, he was a member of the CNAA Education Organization and Management Board and his publications include The Role of the Consultant in Organization Development in *Handbook of Management Training*, McGraw-Hill and Human Resource Development in Western Germany in *Industrial Training International*.

In his mainstream consultancy activities Geoffrey has worked across Europe and in the Far East with several multinational organizations, and for 12 months he acted as Head of Management Training for British Rail, during which time he was active, and still is, in developing links and exchanges between education and industry through industrial projects for schoolteachers.